Ask CosmoGIRL!

About
Beauty

**From the Editors
of CosmoGIRL!**

WITHDRAWN

Ask COSMOgirl!

About Beauty

**From the Editors
of CosmoGIRL!**

HEARST BOOKS

A division of Sterling Publishing Co., Inc.

New York / London
www.sterlingpublishing.com

Library of Congress Cataloging-in-Publication Data
Ask CosmoGIRL! about beauty : all the answers to your questions about hair, makeup, skin & more / from the editors of CosmoGIRL!.
    p. cm.
Includes index.
ISBN-13: 978-1-58816-644-9
ISBN-10: 1-58816-644-9
1. Beauty, Personal. 2. Cosmetics. 3. Teenage girls–Health and hygiene. I. Cosmo girl.
RA778.A833 2008
646.7'2–dc22

10 9 8 7 6 5 4 3 2 1

Book design by Margaret Rubiano

Published by Hearst Books
A Division of Sterling Publishing Co., Inc.
387 Park Avenue South, New York, NY 10016

CosmoGIRL! and Hearst Books are trademarks of
Hearst Communications, Inc.

www.cosmogirl.com

For information about custom editions, special sales,
premium and corporate purchases, please contact
Sterling Special Sales Department at 800-805-5489 or
specialsales@sterlingpublishing.com.

Distributed in Canada by Sterling Publishing
C/o Canadian Manda Group, 165 Dufferin Street
Toronto, Ontario, Canada M6K 3H6

Distributed in Australia by Capricorn Link (Australia) Pty. Ltd.
P.O. Box 704, Windsor, NSW 2756 Australia

Manufactured in China

Sterling ISBN 13: 978-1-58816-644-9
      ISBN 10: 1-58816-644-9

Photo credits:
Nino Muñoz, pg. 10; Alban Christ, pg. 34; Phillippe Salomon, pg. 44; Stephen Lee, pg. 60; Cleo Sullivan, pg. 68; Liz Von Hoene, pg. 78; Fred Aufray, pg. 92; Fred Aufray, pg. 128.

contents

Foreword: Susan's Note 8

Chapter 1: Skin Basics 10

Chapter 2: Hair Removal 34

Chapter 3: Acne Treatment 44

Chapter 4: Cover-Up How-Tos 60

Chapter 5: Healthy Mouth 68

Chapter 6: Eye Makeup How-Tos 78

Chapter 7: Hair Help 92

Chapter 8: Nail Know-How 128

Index 135

foreword

Hey CosmoGIRL!s,

I remember when I was about five years old I had this doll—it was a head and shoulders kind of thing, and it came with make-up and hair accessories so I could play makeup artist/hairstylist on her. Maybe you had the same toy, I think they make a new version of it every ten years! It's just one of those things that little girls like to do—play with makeup and hairstyles. It's fun! As you get older and start having slumber parties, what do you do? You sit around putting makeup on each other and doing each other's hair. Again, because it's fun! And it's something to do while you talk about guys, celebs and gossip in general. But now that you're actually wearing makeup and doing your hair on a daily basis, putting together a real beauty look for yourself can be tricky. All the products and techniques can get a little confusing. What's the best way to put on eyeliner? Which lip color is best for your skin tone? Should you wear foundation or not? For every beauty product out there, there's a question about how to use it correctly or if you should even use it at all! I know, because you write to us every day with your beauty dilemmas. So in this book, we've put together your most-often asked questions so that no matter what the occasion—regular school day, Friday night football game, your best friend's sweet sixteen, whatever—we'll have answers and ideas that you can use to achieve the look you want. That way, you can actually forget about how you look, and focus on living your life. That's really why we wear makeup, right? When you look great, you feel great, and that helps you put your best foot forward in whatever you do. So use this book as a resource whenever you need it. And at the end of the day, remember to have fun! Because as we all learned when we were little girls, that's what beauty is all about.

Send me your beauty questions and ideas whenever you want— I'm here to listen and get you answers at susan@cosmogirl.com

Love,

chapter 1

skin basics

Healthy skin is a hallmark of beauty, and the canvas you "paint" all your other beauty tricks on. But it's not going to stay healthy without your taking care of it! In this chapter, find answers to your top questions about skin care.

skin basics

cleansing tips

Q **I just bought a new cleanser all my friends were raving about, but it doesn't make my skin tingle like my old one did. Don't I have to feel something for a product to be working?**

A Guess what? You don't. Companies make tingly washes and grainy scrubs because research shows that people associate certain sensations with cleanliness. Those products do cleanse but may not clear up pimples. If you like them and they don't bother your skin, go ahead and use them.

Q **Do generic products work as well as brand-name products?**

A In general, yes. Here's how to gauge if a generic product is going to work as well as the pricier brand-name one. If a generic brand (products that have your drugstore's name on them) contains the same active ingredient as the brand-name product and the ingredients list is similar, they will pretty much work the same.

Q **Is the active ingredient all that matters in acne medication?**

A No. Active ingredients are only a part of it; you should also choose the correct formula for your skin type. If your skin is oily, try alcohol-based liquids or gels, which evaporate quickly so your skin doesn't look or feel moist. Got normal to dry skin? Go for lotions or creams, which are lightweight and more moisturizing.

Q **I use four or five products on my face a day—a soap, a scrub, a mask, and zit cream. Is this bad for my skin?**

A If your skin is glowing (and your beauty budget allows you to stock up on tons of stuff), then no, it's not a problem. Younger skin is more resilient than an adult's, so it's hard to overdo it. But if your skin gets flaky, blotchy, or starts breaking out, it's time to scale back. All this product pileup may be irritating your precious face! Believe it or not, simple skincare routines almost always work better than intensive regimens. Try washing every morning with a gentle cleanser. Before bed, wash again and then apply zit cream to flare-ups only. If you go through a beauty product withdrawal, a weekly pore-cleansing mask can give you the boost you're craving. Just wait for your skin to clear up before adding a mask to your lineup.

skin basics

Q What's the difference between a toner and an astringent? Do I need both?

A The general rule is that astringents are alcohol-based while toners are water- or witch-hazel based (so they contain little or no alcohol). However, the names are often used interchangeably, so check the label. If the first ingredient listed is alcohol, it's probably an astringent—even if it's called a toner. Now, for the next part of your question: You definitely don't need a toner *and* an astringent. In fact, if your skin is normal-to-dry, you don't need either. But you might like how it makes your skin feel—refreshed and cleanser-free. If that's the case, it's perfectly okay to use one that's alcohol-free. Swipe a cotton ball with toner or astringent on your face at night (don't overdo it). If you have oily skin and/or you have a tendency to break out, look for a product with either glycolic acid or salicylic acid. Use once in the morning and once again at night. (In your case, it's better to check for one of those ingredients—both to get rid of pore-clogging oil and to slough off dead skin cells without overdrying your skin—than it is to look specifically for a toner or an astringent.) An alcohol-based product without these ingredients can dry out your skin and make breakouts worse.

oily skin

Q **My skin is oily, and my makeup always runs within two hours after applying it! It's so gross! What can I do?**

A After washing your face, smooth mattifying gel onto your forehead, nose, chin, and anywhere else you tend to get oily. Then apply your usual makeup. (The absorbent microbeads in the gel sit on the skin's surface and act like little sponges, soaking up excess oil all day.) To degrease during the day, mist your face with water (keep a little spray bottle in your locker), then blot with a paper towel. The water dissolves oil on your skin's surface. You can also treat problem skin at home with a clay mask that contains sulfur. The clay absorbs excess oil, which will prevent future breakouts, and the sulfur kills bacteria and reduces swelling on existing zits.

CG! TIP: **Apply pressed powder over cream blush. If your complexion feels oily during the day, just dab gently with blotting papers.**

skin basics

Q My skin feels greasy an hour after washing my face. Any suggestions?

A Control oil by using a foaming or gel cleanser in the morning and at night. Avoid using bar soaps and washing your face more than twice daily—both will dry out skin, which causes irritation and may lead to acne. Follow with an alcohol-based toner or astringent. If you're acne-prone, choose one with salicylic or glycolic acid to exfoliate skin, which opens clogged pores. Try an oil-free SPF 15 or 30 sunscreen instead of a moisturizer. Once a month, use a mask with salicylic acid. To conceal pimples, use a dry, powdery concealer. This consistency is best for oily skin and will stay put, as opposed to a creamy one which slips off. To keep concealer from looking streaky, apply it with a synthetic brush, then dab loose powder on top with a sponge.

CG! TIP: Skip heavy makeup when it's hot. Instead, apply a light, tinted moisturizer to even out skin tone.

combination skin

Q **My nose and forehead get shiny during the day, but the skin around my mouth, eyes, and cheeks is on the dry side. How can I treat my skin if I don't know whether it's dry or oily?**

A Wash your face in the morning and at night with a foaming cleanser. Your skin shouldn't feel tight when you're done washing it. At night, use an alcohol free toner with salicylic or glycolic acid all over your face, or, if your cheeks feel dry, just on your forehead, nose, and chin. This kind of toner is essential since the acid clears up pores and prevents pimples without drying out skin. Use a nonmedicated scrub, one made of natural ingredients like papaya or mango seeds to treat skin weekly. If you're acne prone, it'll provide the extra exfoliation you need to stop red, inflamed pimples from forming. To cover up existing blemishes, use a creamy foundation as concealer. Thick concealer may crack on drier spots. Use a lip brush to apply it with precision. If one coat doesn't cover the pimple, apply a second layer, then set with translucent powder.

CG! TIP: **To treat dry, irritated skin, try a moisturizing body wash instead of regular bar soap.**

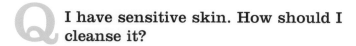

sensitive skin

Q **I have sensitive skin. How should I cleanse it?**

A Avoid products that can irritate your skin, such as those containing benzoyl peroxide. Instead, wash with a gentle, soap-free moisturizing cleanser and prevent pimples by applying a product that contains salicylic acid at night to acne-prone areas. Use just a dab wherever you tend to get whiteheads, blackheads, or red bumps. If using it daily makes your skin sting or turn red, cut back to every other day. In the morning, finish by applying a broad-spectrum SPF 15 or SPF 30 moisturizer with zinc or titanium dioxide, chemical-free ingredients that won't irritate skin. Acne-prone? Use a nonmedicated scrub once a week. If you're ultrasensitive, scrub only monthly. If you have blotchy or uneven coloring, use a tinted moisturizer for an overall flawless finish. Then conceal pimples by mixing the tinted moisturizer with a creamy concealer. Apply with a clean lip brush and apply a thin layer of the mixture directly onto your pimples.

CG! TIP: **Makeup brushes harbor bacteria if you don't keep them clean. Wash them weekly with a mild soap and let air-dry.**

Q I'm African-American, and my skin can be very sensitive sometimes. Do you have any special recommendations for my complexion?

A Wash with a benzoyl peroxide cleanser every day. Avoid products with salicylic acid; it can irritate sensitive skin. Treat remaining pimples with a benzoyl peroxide cream. Doctors aren't sure why, but African-American skin scars worse from acne than other skin types do. Apply a cream with a fading ingredient to acne scars twice a day for at least three months. Because the sun can darken scars, wear SPF 30 sunscreen every day, and if you're in the sun for longer than 30 minutes, reapply every two hours.

Didja Know?
Skin of color is often more sensitive and needs special care.

skin basics

scar prevention

Q I recently got a bad burn on my leg, and I'm afraid it's going to scar. How can I stop that from happening?

A First, look at the burn. If it's not blistering and feels like a sunburn, you can treat it on your own. (If it is blistering, or if the skin is loose, go to a doctor. It's likely a deep second- or third-degree burn, which needs special care.) Now, despite what you may have heard, you should never put butter on a burn—it can cause infection, which can lead to scarring. Instead, run cold water over the burn for at least 30 minutes. This will reduce swelling and will minimize the risk of scarring. Applying an antibiotic ointment can also help prevent infection. Cover the burn loosely with gauze once a day or whenever it gets wet. If the scab peels as it's healing—don't pick it! Picking can cause scarring. If you notice an infection (symptoms include red streaks, swelling, pus, odor, or fever), go to your doctor right away—you need an antibiotic. Once the wound has healed (there's no scab and it's completely dry), start using a vitamin E cream or cocoa butter twice a day. And from now on, apply sunscreen (SPF 30 or higher) when outdoors.

Q I'm African-American, and I had acne in my early teens. Now I have dark spots where my breakouts used to be. Is there anything I can do?

A When you get a pimple or pick at one, pigment cells (which give skin its color) go into overdrive, producing extra pigment that goes deeper into your skin. But the pigment often spreads into surrounding skin cells, producing a dark spot. You can treat the spots by applying a lotion once a day that contains salicylic acid, but it probably isn't strong enough to fade the spots completely. The best thing to do is to see your dermatologist. She can prescribe Retin-A, Differin, or Tazorac, all of which can fade the dark pigment safely. Warning: Never try to lighten spots with an over-the-counter cream that claims it will "fade," "bleach," or "whiten" your skin. Those creams contain hydroquinone, which is strong enough to lighten the skin around dark spots but not the dark spots themselves—so in the end, they'll stand out even more.

skin basics

Q How can I get rid of a hickey?

A A hickey is basically a bruise, so to make it go away, treat it like you would a bruise. Coat the hickey with aloe vera, then rub it in with the back of a frozen spoon (just pop a spoon in the freezer for a half hour) for 10 minutes daily to speed fading. The icy spoon will help constrict blood vessels, so there's less bleeding under the skin; the aloe helps reduce inflammation.

CG! TIP: **Eat healthy fats that are found in nuts, fish, and olive oil. They nourish cells and make skin glow.**

large pores

Q **What's the best way to shrink the pores on my nose or cover them up? Is there a skin product that will help make them look less noticeable?**

A Your pores are probably larger because the sebum (a fatty secretion of the sebaceous gland) packed deep inside them makes pore shafts widen. Exfoliate three times a week to remove the sebum. Then, spread a pore minimizing gel over your nose before putting on makeup—it will help tighten pores so your makeup doesn't sink into them. You can also reduce pore size by swiping your entire face every morning with a salicylic acid or glycolic acid toner—both act as exfoliators and dissolve dirt and oil deep inside your pores. Spot treat (so that your healthy skin won't get too dried out) only your largest pores two or three times a week with a product that contains sulfur. Just dab it on and let the product sit for 5 to 10 minutes. Then rinse your face with warm water.

skin basics

lines and wrinkles

Q I can already see fine lines appearing around my eyes and between my eyebrows, and it really bothers me. Is it a good idea to use an anti-wrinkle cream?

A First off, you may think your lines are obvious—but trust us, other people will probably look at you and say, "What lines?" That said, it's always a good idea to give your undereye area a little TLC. The skin there is the thinnest on your whole body, and it doesn't produce enough oil to keep it naturally moisturized, which is why wrinkles often appear there first. To give this area the moisture it needs, look for a light lotion or gel that contains Vitamin C—it should say so on the package. Vitamin C can help reduce fine lines, which are often the result of sun damage (a primary cause of wrinkles). Just dot a pea-sized amount under your eyes and between your brows every night (don't rub—that can irritate the skin). You have to protect your face and undereye area during the day too—apply sunblock with at least SPF 15 every morning, and wear sunglasses that have both UVA and UVB protection when you're outside.

stretch marks

Q **I have these red lines on my breasts, and I don't know how they got there. Are they normal? Will they go away?**

A Sounds like you have stretch marks. A lot of us get them as teens because our breasts are growing faster than the skin around them, and so the layers of tissue in the skin are stretched thin, says Karyn Grossman, M.D., a dermatologist who has offices in New York and Los Angeles. The marks are red because deeper layers of skin tear and then swell. Within a year, however, they'll turn white and fade as the inflammation goes away. If you are African-American, do not use bleaching creams to get rid of stretch marks. Bleaching creams can lighten skin pigmentation but they won't fade stretch marks. You can have a dermatologist lighten them with a laser—but it's expensive and you'll need about three to five visits. Just remember: Stretch marks are entirely normal and the majority of girls have them—so before you do anything drastic, just know that you're not alone!

skin basics

sun and your skin

Q I always stay out of the sun, but I love being tan. Are indoor tanning beds less dangerous?

A When tanning beds first became popular, scientists thought UVB rays (which cause skin to redden) were more dangerous than UVA rays. So manufacturers made beds that emitted fewer UVB rays and more UVA rays. Now scientists believe UVA rays may be more dangerous because they penetrate deeper, causing wrinkles and possibly cancer. The verdict? Avoid the tanning salon. You get the same harmful rays from the tanning bed that you do from the sun. Instead, try a spray tan. You'll get a golden glow without the harmful effects of the sun!

Didja Know?
Deodorant doesn't work as well if your skin is damp—so before applying, blow-dry your armpits for two seconds.

Q If I start out with a base tan, can I prevent sunburn?

A No. Even though your skin *looks* darker, you can still burn. Also, a base tan (whether from a tanning bed or the sun) doesn't provide protection like sunscreen. Getting a tan and then lying out in the sun doubles your exposure—and increases your risk of skin cancer. Bottom line? A tan means you've damaged your skin. No tan is healthy, despite what society views as "healthy."

Q I've heard it's not bad to sunbathe if you only do it once in a while. Is this true?

A Not really. A tan may fade, but its irreversible damage doesn't: UV rays break down collagen and elastin (components of the skin that prevent it from sagging and looking wrinkly). Because UV damage is cumulative, the more you tan, the earlier you'll start to wrinkle and increase your chances of getting skin cancer. In the last decade, cases of melanoma, the deadliest form of skin cancer, have increased 20 percent among women ages 15 to 34.

skin basics

Q Does tanning clear up acne?

A A tan might make pimples less noticeable, but it doesn't clear them up. In fact, doctors say tanning can cause pores to look bigger and makes acne even worse. Why? Tanning dehydrates skin, causing it to produce more oil, which can clog pores and lead to more pimples. UV rays also dry out your skin, initially making zits go away, but it's only temporary.

> **Didja Know?**
> Cigarette ads used to say
> smoking was harmless! Sounds crazy,
> right? Now we know better. Think of
> tanning in the same way. It's bad for
> your skin, so start avoiding it today.

Can I still use my sunscreen from last year?

A Probably not. Sunscreen only maintains its effectiveness for six months to a year, so throw out your bottle after the expiration date listed on the bottom. If there's no date, buy a new sunscreen and write the purchase date on the bottom of the bottle. Also, don't keep sunscreen in the car; when sunscreen is exposed to prolonged heat, it loses its effectiveness. Don't spread sunscreen on too thinly, either. You won't get adequate protection. Use an ounce of lotion—a golf-ball-sized amount—or one-quarter of a 4-ounce spray bottle to cover your whole body. Once you get a tan, don't use a sunscreen with a lower SPF. Remember: A tan doesn't protect you from the sun. You can still burn and you still damage your skin even if you can't see it. Use an SPF of at least 30 all summer long. Just because you apply a high SPF doesn't mean you won't have to reapply it: sunscreen starts to break down the second it's in the sun, so no matter what SPF you use, you need to reapply it every two hours. Sunscreen takes 30 minutes to be absorbed, so don't wait until you're already outside before you apply it. Slather it on at home before you get dressed so you won't miss any spots and it will have time to soak in.

self-tanner how-to's

Q I'd like to stay out of the sun, but I hate self-tanners. They stain my clothes! How can I get a tan without having to buy a new wardrobe?

A Switch to a fast-drying aerosol tanner; it soaks into skin faster than lotions, so it won't get absorbed by your clothes. Or, apply your self-tanner 30 minutes before bed. Immediately and thoroughly wash your hands after applying. Then put on an old pair of pj's—think of them as your self-tanner pj's. If they get a little orange, it won't matter. When you wake up the next morning, you'll have the color you want without having ruined any of your clothes.

CG! TIP: **After applying sunscreen, use a cream blush instead of a powder. Powders can look clumpy when applied on top of lotion.**

Q I used sunless tanning lotion, and it stained my hands! How can I get it off?

A Squeeze an exfoliating scrub onto wet palms. Rub your hands together for a minute, then rinse off. Next, cut one slice of lemon and squeeze the juice onto your palms. Rub your hands together for another minute, then wash with soap and water. The scrub helps the self-tanner wash off faster, and lemon juice fades the color. Do this once a day until your hands are back to normal (it'll take about two days). And the next time you self-tan, make sure to wash your hands thoroughly with soap and water after applying!

Q My skin looks all blotchy after I self-tan. How can I avoid that?

A Self-tanner is a pigment that attaches to your top layer of skin, so you need to even out that top layer before you apply the product. Exfoliate skin (which will even out the top layer) and then apply self-tanner. Stay undressed for at least 15 minutes to let the self-tanner dry (fabric can absorb tanner and cause uneven streaks). If your skin still looks blotchy, use a tinted, shimmery body lotion to mask any imperfections.

skin basics

Q **Self-tanners turn my fair skin carrot-orange. How do I choose the right color?**

A Try a gradual self-tanning lotion—which is a blend of moisturizer and self-tanner. When applied daily, it slowly builds up the color, giving your skin a natural-looking tan. Or pick a regular self-tanner that is white or clear when it comes out of the bottle—those usually contain lower levels of the tanning agent DHA so it won't develop too darkly. It's always smart to patch-test the back of your wrist before slathering self-tanner all over.

Q **My self-tanner has a smell that lasts all day. How can I make it go away?**

A You're smelling DHA, the ingredient in most self-tanners that colors your skin. As it develops, it reacts with your skin and causes it to smell. Try applying self-tanner at night and showering the next morning—that should help reduce the odor a bit. Don't exfoliate, however, because you'll scrub off the tan. Also, try mixing lotion-based tanner with a quarter-sized blob of fragrance-free body lotion—it'll dilute the tanner and make the scent less powerful.

How do supermodels get their skin to look so shimmery?

A Sabrina B. Paul (the makeup artist who gives Guess models their sexy look) told us all her tricks. The night before a shoot, the models exfoliate their bodies by showering with a washcloth. Paul then applies two coats of self-tanner to their bodies. (We recommend bronzing your face too.) The next morning, she puts oil-free moisturizer all over the girls' faces. While it's still sinking in, she blends a peachy cream blush onto the apples of their cheeks to create a dewy glow. For extra shine, she uses a shimmery stick highlighter on their cheekbones, brow bones, the tips of their noses, their chins, and then blends. She finishes the look with a coat of bronze shimmer cream on the models' arms, legs, and stomach— any part of the body where the skin will be visible.

CG! TIP: If you break out during the summer, switch to a mineral-based foundation that doesn't contain oil or preservatives, which can cause pimples.

chapter 2

hair removal

Let's face it: It's a necessary evil to get rid of
unwanted hair. Some of us have more or less than
others, but it's always a hassle. Read on to find out
how your fellow CG!s manage their own hair issues.

hair removal

heavy growth

Q **I have a lot of hair covering my body. What can I do?**

A How you get rid of it depends on where it is. For the hair that grows on your chest and nipples, pluck the strays. If you have a lot, try a depilatory. The skin is very sensitive here, so patch-test and use a pinhead-sized amount only on each hair. For your tummy, cold wax will give you a long time between removal and regrowth (four to seven days), but you can also use a depilatory cream. Avoid shaving because stubble can be darker and coarser in this area. For your bikini line, wax fine hair. Before you do, trim the hair you want removed to minimize the pain, then sprinkle on baby powder (to absorb perspiration and oils before you wax). If your bikini-line hair is coarse, shave in the direction your hair grows. As for your toes? Wax those babies!

arm hair

Q I shaved my arms, and my friend told me the hair would grow back stubbly. Is that really true?

A The bad news is that your friend is right. According to New York City dermatologist Debar Jaliman, the hair will grow back prickly because you've sliced off its naturally soft, tapered ends. In about a month, however, the ends will taper off again. (Know how the ends of the hair on your head get thinner as they get longer? Same idea.) To avoid stubble in the future, we recommend a salon waxing. Waxing pulls hair out at the root, which means it will grow back soft (no stubble), and the results will last about three weeks. But if the mere thought of waxing scares you, then a depilatory is probably more your speed. A depilatory dissolves hair under the skin's surface, leaving you with a smooth arm. Your hair will come in softer, but expect further growth sooner than if you waxed—in about two to three days.

facial hair

Q I have a lot of facial hair. What will get rid of it—with no side effects?

A Nothing yet. Electrolysis (where tiny volts of electricity are shot into the hair follicle, killing the growth) and lasering are both permanent, but both also have downsides. They can be painful; they may cause redness for a few days; and they'll cost you big bucks (at least $100 per session). A cheaper option? Waxing. It's possible to wax at home, but first-timers should go to a salon to see how it's done. Waxing produces results that last three to four weeks. There are also prescription-only creams that slow hair growth (you just need to apply them every day.) But before you try any of these tactics, make sure a health problem isn't to blame by visiting your doctor.

CG! TIP: If unwanted facial hair is fine, not coarse, just bleach it.

bikini line

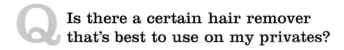

Q Is there a certain hair remover that's best to use on my privates?

A Shaving or using a chemical depilatory are fine for removing any pubic hair you can see while wearing a swimsuit. But if by "privates" you're talking about the area between your legs, then you should see a professional. The skin close to your vagina is very sensitive. At the salon, they'll use wax to take off as much hair as you want (expect to pay $30 or more). But be warned: Though it's safe, waxing there can be painful.

> CG! TIP: **Rub a thin layer of aloe vera on your bikini line the day *after* you shave or wax. It'll keep skin soft, which helps prevent ingrown hairs.**

hair removal

Q **Is shaving off all of my pubic hair a health risk or unsafe in any way?**

A Before you make a date with your razor, you should know that pubic hair is there for a few good health reasons. It provides a cushion that helps prevent your labia (the fleshy skin around your vagina) from getting chafed, which can happen when you wear tight clothes or even ride a bike. The hairs also act sort of like a spiderweb, trapping harmful bacteria so they can't get into your vagina and cause infections like vaginosis. Plus, urinary tract infections are often caused by bacteria from the anus—and if you have no pubic hair, there's a clear pathway for that bacteria to travel to your urethra (where you urinate from) and infect it. Shaving also poses a risk of ingrown hairs (hairs that curl back on themselves and get stuck under the skin, causing sore, painful bumps). There's also the problem of using a sharp blade in a sensitive area that you can't see very well. If you nick yourself while shaving, bacteria could get into the cut and cause a rash. If you still want to shave, follow these steps: (1) Soften hair with warm water; (2) Apply plenty of shaving cream; (3) Use a brand-new razor; and lastly, (4) Shave gently in the direction that the pubic hair grows. Another option is waxing—which you should let a professional do. A salon can take it all off (a Brazilian wax) for $30 to $50. One final warning: Keep depilatories like Nair away from your genitals. The chemicals can burn your labia.

razor burn

Q **I just shaved and now my skin is covered in painful red bumps. What is this—and what can I do about it?**

A You have razor burn! But don't worry—it's easily treated. Rub an over the counter hydrocortisone cream on the bumps daily, and don't shave again until they're gone (it'll take two to three days). Hydrocortisone is a natural anti-inflammatory that reduces redness and irritation. Next time you shave, stand in the shower at least five minutes before shaving. The warmth and moisture softens hair so it is easier to shave and hair follicles are less likely to get irritated. Make sure your razor isn't too dull—it can cause nicks. And always use moisturizing shave gel or cream—shaving without lubrication causes razor burn. In the meantime, hide red bumps by dabbing on concealer (the same one you use on your face).

pit pitfalls

Q I shaved my armpits, and now they're all itchy, bumpy, and red. Please help!

A You probably had an allergic reaction to your shave gel or deodorant (especially if you recently tried a new brand) or you didn't wet down your underarms enough before shaving (shaving dry skin can cause irritation). First, apply a cool compress for five to ten minutes—it'll soothe the swelling. Now tackle the itchy, red bumps by dabbing on a thin layer of hydrocortisone cream. Do it once in the morning and once before you go to bed until the bumps disappear. If they're not gone in a week, see a dermatologist. In the meantime, you can still shave your armpits and wear deodorant—just use products labeled "for sensitive skin."

Q My underarms have a dark, shadow-like appearance! It's embarrassing—I can't wear cute tank tops.

A You're probably being too rough on your underarms. Irritating the delicate skin can result in post-inflammatory hyperpigmentation (your skin reacts to irritation by darkening). Shaving, rubbing on deodorant harshly, or allergies to product ingredients can all cause irritation. To stop the irritation and let your underarms return to normal, try to shave less frequently for a month, and always use products for sensitive skin when you do shave. Thoroughly wet your underarms and apply shaving cream. Then shave from the top of your armpit to the bottom. Finish by using a gel deodorant, which glides on gently (unlike a solid stick, which can be rougher). If you don't notice improvement after a month, see a dermatologist.

chapter 3

acne treatment

Don't you hate it when you've got something special planned, and your skin suddenly breaks out? You're not alone. See what some of your fellow CG!s have to say about those pesky pimples, and learn how to prevent them in the future.

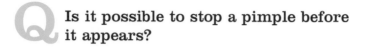

pimple prevention

Q **Is it possible to stop a pimple before it appears?**

A Yes, but you have to catch it in time. As soon as you feel a pimple forming, dip a Q-tip in hydrogen peroxide and dab it on the pimple twice a day until it heals (do not pick at it). This should take about two to three days. The peroxide will kill the active bacteria, and its bleaching component will diminish redness.

Q **How can I avoid painful pimples before and after my period?**

A Daily prevention is the key. If you wait to treat the pimples until your period starts, you won't be able to do much. Wash your face every morning and night with a 2 percent salicylic acid cleanser. The acid exfoliates your skin, as well as dissolves dirt and oil to prevent big zits from forming. If you still get painful pimples, apply a 5 to 10 percent benzoyl peroxide cream. It's an anti-inflammatory and will make your zits smaller by the next morning. Remember: No picking, popping, or squeezing, all of which spread bacteria and make pimples more inflamed.

acne remedies

 How do acne-fighting products actually work?

A Benzoyl peroxide kills the bacteria inside your pimples and helps reduce inflammation so your zits won't hurt as badly (or look as red). Salicylic acid is great for mild acne. It exfoliates dead skin and dirt to unclog your pores and it works well in combination with benzoyl peroxide. Glycolic acid is similar to salicylic acid, but it's stronger. Used with benzoyl peroxide, it can be effective on moderate cases of acne. Sulfur's benefits are similar to those of benzoyl peroxide—it reduces swelling and dries up oil. But it's not an antibacterial. It can work great on large pores and hard zits.

acne treatment

Q **I've seen a lot of new products with tea tree oil. What is it good for?**

A Tea tree oil has all kinds of great purposes, says Scott Dinehart, an associate professor of dermatology at the University of Arkansas. Most common purpose? It's used to fight acne. When you put it on a pimple, it reduces redness, deflates bumps, and keeps small pimples from becoming big, nasty ones. Tea tree oil also fights athlete's foot, soothes an itchy scalp (look for it in shampoos and conditioners), and deep-cleans oily skin. A downside? Pure tea tree oil can be irritating (some people are allergic to it), so if you're a first-time user, do a patch test. Apply the oil to the inside of your arm, wait 24 hours, then if you don't have a reaction, go ahead and use it elsewhere.

Q I have mild acne but I don't want to see a dermatologist for it. Is there anything you can recommend to treat it?

A Wash your face every other night with a 2 percent salicylic acid wash. The cleanser will exfoliate and clean your skin. Every day, apply an oil-free lotion to hydrate skin. If you still have whiteheads or blackheads after six weeks, try using a retinoid product—it will unclog pores and keep them clear. To treat any stubborn red bumps, apply a pea-sized amount of a 5 percent benzoyl peroxide or cream gel over the affected area every other morning. Gradually work up to once daily (so you don't dry out your skin) until the bumps are gone.

Q I have really bad acne. Is there any over-the-counter remedy you can recommend?

A You may have to see a dermatologist because over-the-counter products may not be able to help severe acne. But here's something you can try: To reduce inflammation of cystic pimples, put a dab of hydrocortisone cream on the tip of a cotton swab and apply to the zit once daily. The cortisone will help reduce the redness and swelling. Warning: Apply it only to the pimple itself—not the skin around it—or you'll dry out your face!

acne treatment

Q **How do I get rid of my acne without drying out my skin?**

A You should ease into your skincare regimen—using too many acne products at once sucks moisture from your face. If you have dry or sensitive skin, start by washing your face twice a day with a basic cleanser. For oily skin, try a cleanser with a low concentration (2 percent or less) of benzoyl peroxide or salicylic acid. Then use a cotton swab to apply a 2 percent salicylic acid cream to spot-treat a breakout. If your face feels dry, apply a pea-sized drop of oil-free moisturizer all over it.

Q **I just started a new pimple treatment—when will I see results?**

A Most of the time, you need to wait six weeks to see if a product is working on your skin. Some companies don't put this fact on product labels because they're concerned you'll think six weeks is too long to wait and that it will discourage you from buying the product.

Q Isn't more pimple cream better than less?

A In general, active ingredients such as benzoyl peroxide (the most effective over-the-counter ingredient used to treat acne) and salicylic acid can irritate or dry skin. Try the lowest percentage of those ingredients you can find—usually 2.5 percent for benzoyl peroxide and 0.5 percent for salicylic acid. If you don't see improvement after six weeks, try a product with a higher percentage of the active ingredient.

CG! TIP: **Acne products make your skin highly susceptible to sunburn, so wear SPF 30 sunscreen at all times.**

acne treatment

Q **Is it true that toothpaste makes your zits go away? My friends swear by it.**

A Actually, it can, yes. This is one of those old wives' tales that does work, says New York City dermatologist Peter Wisch. Creamy toothpastes (not the gel kind) act sort of like a clay mask (think about how it hardens if you drop a splotch on your sink and forget to wipe it off), which draws dirt and oil out of your pores. But before you stock up, Wisch also says that toothpaste should never be your first defense against pimples. In other words, if you're stuck in a log cabin deep in the woods for a week and a pimple crops up, then it's okay to pat on a pinhead-sized dab of toothpaste. But if you have access to a drugstore, you're better off buying an acne treatment. A splotch of toothpaste may temporarily dry up a pimple, but it's not going to be a long-term fix.

Q Help! I'm 15 years old and have been breaking out for two years! My mom keeps telling me "it's just a phase." How can I tell her that this is ruining my life?

A Your mom probably knows all too well what you're going through, but as it's been years since she's gone through it herself, she may just need a gentle reminder about what it's like to be a teenager with acne. We suggest that you arrange to have a special mother-daughter chat. Present the facts: Let her know that untreated acne can cause physical scars, plus permanent damage to your self-esteem and confidence. Also, this "phase" could last well into your 30s! And don't forget to remind her how she felt when she was a teenager (chances are, if you've got acne, so did she).

acne treatment

quick fixes

Q **I have a huge pimple on my nose and I have to go to a party tomorrow. Help!**

A "If you're not allergic to aspirin, take one," says Howard Murad, M.D. It's an anti-inflammatory, so it'll help soothe and shrink the bump. (Note: This trick is for red and painful pimple emergencies only. Don't pop an aspirin every time you get one.) Then apply a cool compress (like a damp washcloth) to the pimple for five minutes. Attack the bump overnight by dotting a sulfur-based spot treatment on clean skin. The day of the party, take an aspirin in the morning and reapply your compress. Dab concealer on the tip of the pimple and gently blend. Use a Q-tip to dab powder over your blemish, which will soak up any oil and help the concealer stay put.

I just picked a pimple and now it's oozing. Any advice?

A After you've picked a pimple, wrap an ice cube in a paper towel and press it on the spot for five minutes—it'll reduce the redness. Then dab a damp styptic pencil—one of those white sticks guys use to stop shaving cuts from bleeding—over it. It has ingredients that stop bleeding and oozing. If the skin is not open (as in, peeled away), hide the spot with a concealer that has salicylic acid, which helps the pimple heal. If it is open, skip the concealer—it won't go on smoothly over a surface that's been picked, and you'll only end up with an uneven mess. If you're at school when this happens, go to the bathroom and press a piece of paper towel on the spot for two to three minutes. This should stop the oozing.

Didja Know?
In 17th-century England, women applied egg whites to their faces to tighten their skin and give them a glow.

---

stubborn acne

Q **I have all these pimples on my forehead, and nothing gets rid of them. Any suggestions?**

A You're probably already using a cleanser with salicylic acid and applying pimple-fighting cream at night, so we won't bore you to tears by telling you to do it again. What you really need to do is find out if you have any habits that could be contributing to the pimples. Here's a quick checklist: Do you rest your forehead on your arm when you're in class? Do you use styling cream, wax, or hairspray? Do you wear hats? If you said yes to any of these, you can help prevent your pimples. Don't rest your forehead on your arm or touch it with your fingers—this way you're not contributing to the clogging. As for styling products, don't use waxes or creams on your bangs (or on the hair near your forehead). They have oils that clog your pores and cause breakouts. When you use hairspray, shield your forehead with one hand so it doesn't hit your skin. It's also important to wash your pillowcase once a week—it can harbor breakout-causing oils. If you do all this and still don't notice a change after six weeks, see a dermatologist. She can prescribe an antibiotic cream or give you a personal skincare regimen.

banishing blackheads

 I have blackheads in my ears. Help!

A Blackheads are pores clogged with oil. When the oil is exposed to air and bacteria, it becomes oxidized and turns black. The best way to get rid of blackheads is to have them removed by a dermatologist with a special tool called a comedone extractor. (Don't try it on your own—you could damage your inner ear.) It puts pressure around all sides of the blackhead, which pushes the oil out. But don't worry: It shouldn't hurt. After the blackheads have been extracted, apply a product with glycolic acid to your ears every night to keep new blackheads from forming. Even if you decide not to see a dermatologist, you can still use a product with glycolic acid to clean out your pores. You should see results in one to two weeks.

body breakouts

Q I sometimes get pimple-like bumps on my chest. What causes them and what can I use to get rid of them?

A It's hard to say without seeing them, but your bumps could be caused by too much sun exposure or excessive sweating. If they show up right after you spend time in the sun and they sting or itch, it could be an allergic reaction. Applying a thin layer of at least 1 percent hydrocortisone cream over the area three times a day should stop the itch and keep the swelling down. If the bumps look and feel like face acne, a cleanser containing 10 percent benzoyl peroxide will help dry out the oil that's causing the breakouts. Squirt some on your palms or on a *white* washcloth (benzoyl peroxide bleaches colored fabrics), and wash the area in the shower. Treat stubborn acne areas with 2 percent salicylic acid acne wipes. If the bumps stick around for more than two weeks, see a dermatologist.

Q I have acne on my shoulders and back. The prom is coming up next month and I wanted to wear a strapless gown, but how can I when I have these ugly bumps all over me?

A These tips will get your bod bump-free in no time. Spot-treat any pimples with a 10 percent benzoyl peroxide gel. It will help kill bacteria inside your pores and make pimples (and any redness) shrink fast. Wash your breakout-prone body parts once daily with an acne body wash. Most contain salicylic acid, which unclogs pores and helps prevent new pimples from forming. Another trick: Take off exercise clothes as soon as you finish your workout. Sweat-soaked fabric can irritate pores and cause pimples. Don't take any chances—pack a dry T-shirt to wear until you can shower.

chapter 4

cover-up how-tos

Most of us don't have perfect skin, but you can get a
smooth look with the right makeup products. Here's
some advice we've given to other CosmoGIRL!s.

foundation basics

Q **My skin is really pale. When I wear foundation, my face doesn't match my neck. What can I do?**

A What you need is a sheer face color, says New York City makeup artist Morgen Schick. She suggests warming up your skin tone first by using a tinted moisturizer or a very light (that's light as in consistency, not color) foundation and applying it with a cosmetic sponge to your face and neck. Then use a big, fluffy blush brush to dust translucent face powder in the same area (the powder will make the moisturizer or foundation last all day without adding extra color). Then, as a final step, apply a dab of pink oil-free gel blush to the apples of your cheeks (rub it in gently with your fingertips) to give your skin the extra glow you're after.

Q **I'm Asian, so it's hard to find a foundation, powder, and concealer that are right for my skin tone. Any suggestions?**

A Look for yellow-based makeup, which will blend most naturally, says celeb makeup artist Mally Roncal (who's also Asian). Yellow-based makeup should look neutral, not warm (orangey) or cool (bluish or pinkish). Once you've narrowed down your picks, match the shades to your neck instead of your hands and face (they can be blotchy, not smooth and even like your neck, so you might not get a perfect match). Another option is to have your makeup custom-blended. It's pricey, but you're guaranteed an exact match! One more tip: Skip translucent powder (it looks white and ashy on Asian skin). Either go for powder in the same shade as your foundation and concealer, or skip it and just blot your skin to soak up extra oil.

Didja Know?
Storing your lipsticks and fragrances in the fridge will make them last longer.

undereye circles

Q **I have dark circles around my eyes. How can I make them look normal?**

A If your dark circles don't disappear after eight hours of beauty sleep, they're likely the result of genetics. Sometimes blood vessels sit closer to the skin's surface (making it appear purple). Because they're part of your DNA, you can't make them disappear completely but you *can* lighten them a little. Finger-pat the circle with a yellowish concealer that's one shade lighter than your skin tone. Then dab loose powder on top to make the cream stay put. Circles, be gone!

CG! TIP: Perfect your complexion in seconds by dabbing foundation over your eyelids to even out skin tone and around your nostrils to cover redness.

acne scars

Q My acne scars are bothering me. Are there any products that will hide them?

A The good news is that people don't notice your scars as much as you think they do. But since they make you feel self-conscious, here's some advice: To disguise flat, discolored spots, we suggest you dab them with a concealer that matches your skin tone. For pockmarks (aka indents), cover them with a light-diffusing highlighting stick. The microscopic "mirrors" blur the indents and make skin look smoother. And if the scars are raised, skip concealer and just smooth on a thin layer of sheer foundation (thicker makeup will make the bumps appear bigger).

Didja Know?
Doctors are developing new laser light treatments to fight acne scars. Visit aad.org for more info.

cover-up how-tos

sunburn Rx

Q I got too much sun this weekend and I can't go to school looking like a lobster. What can I do?

A To subdue a sunburn, use your middle finger to blend a creamy concealer with peach undertones over red areas like the brow bone, cheeks, and the bridge of your nose. Peach reduces redness but looks more natural than a stand-alone concealer, which can be too pale if you have a sunburn.

freckle face

 How can I hide my freckles without using a ton of makeup?

A One day we hope you'll come to love those freckles! In the meantime, try these tips. Prevent your freckles from getting darker or multiplying by wearing sunblock of at least SPF 15 under your makeup every day. Then conceal your freckles by using a highly pigmented, lightweight liquid foundation. Choose a color that's very close to (or just slightly darker than) your skin tone. Using a sponge, blend a layer of the foundation all over your face—from your hairline to your jawline. Then dust on a layer of translucent powder to set it. But just because you now know how to hide your freckles doesn't mean you *should* hide them. Even if you don't see it, freckles are adorable.

chapter 5

healthy mouth

A perfect pout can be difficult to achieve. Here are
some of the issues you've had with your teeth and lips—
and solutions we've given to make yours polished
and prctty!

bad teeth Rx

Q I don't like the appearance of my teeth and I want to fix them. How do I go about doing this?

A Are your teeth crooked or stained? The good news is that there are options available to correct this. Veneers are used mostly for badly stained or crooked teeth. With this procedure, a dentist shaves a little off the edges of each problematic tooth so custom-made teeth can be bonded on top of the natural ones. This costs about $900 to $2,500 per tooth, but veneers can last 10 to 20 years. Lumineers, which are best for lightly stained, slightly crooked, or chipped teeth, are a thinner type of veneer (each is about as thick as a contact lens), so the dentist doesn't need to alter your natural teeth. Because they're thin, they do have to be replaced every five to seven years, and cost about $700 to $1,200 per tooth. Bonding is best for straight but slightly gapped teeth. In this procedure, a dentist etches marks into your tooth's enamel so a plastic-like filler can stick to it. A light is then used to set the filler into its desired shape. It's $300 to $1,000 per tooth, but lasts 5 to 11 years.

floss first

Q What can I do to keep my mouth healthy?

 Always floss before brushing. Food and bacteria get trapped between gums and teeth, which can cause gum disease. So floss twice daily, then brush for two minutes. Also use an alcohol free mouthwash in the morning and at night (alcohol-based mouthwashes can damage your tooth enamel over time).

bright smile

Q **I use whitening toothpaste every single day, but my teeth are still yellow. Help!**

A Have you been to the dentist lately? Whitening toothpaste alone can't make up for neglecting your pearly, um, soon-to-be whites. A good cleaning will at least remove surface stains (from discolorers like soda and coffee), says Larry Rosenthal, D.D.S., director of the Rosenthal Group for Aesthetic Dentistry in New York City. And while you're in the chair, ask your dentist about available whitening services. In-office treatments, which use strong bleaching agents, are the most effective (the results can last up to 18 months). But they're not cheap—think $500 to $1,000. Do-it-yourself kits (available for $11 to $60) may work too, but check with your dentist first. Results can vary and a bad bleach job can damage your enamel.

CG! TIP: **Yellow teeth? Cut down on notorious teeth stainers like coffee and soda. Also, try using a toothpaste with baking soda and hydrogen peroxide.**

brilliant braces

Q I need braces, but my parents couldn't afford them when I was younger. Is 17 too old to get braces?

A You're never too old for braces. Most people get braces when they're younger just to get it over with. But since you're a little older, you'll probably be better at following the orthodontist's orders, so your teeth will turn out great. You should see an orthodontist covered by your dental insurance plan for a consultation. She can analyze your teeth and offer various options (there are now clear appliance trays and porcelain brackets—both are less noticeable than some of the older options). Depending on your insurance coverage, prices will vary. Get a second opinion, however, to make sure you're doing the right thing.

lip trick

Q **My lips are so thin. How can I make them look fuller without using a ton of gloss?**

A To make lips look fuller, rub a champagne-colored powder eye shadow at the center of each lip, then apply a clear gloss. The shadow is paler than your natural lip color, so it creates a highlight. You can also make them look more full by applying a lip balm before gloss—it fills out the tiny cracks in your lips, creating a full, smooth surface.

CG! TIP: **To prevent chapped lips, use lip balm year-round—and be sure to use one that offers UV protection.**

chapped lips

Q **I have severely chapped lips. What can I do?**

A In the morning, wet your lips with water, then exfoliate any dead skin by gently rubbing a damp washcloth or baby toothbrush over them (don't use your regular toothbrush—the bristles are too hard). Then apply a lip balm with sunscreen. Finish by using a colored lip gloss but avoid matte lipsticks, which dry out lips and create flakes. Always remember to drink plenty of water—lips dry out when your body's dehydrated.

CG! TIP: **Apply lip balm before makeup. This gives it time to sink in and condition so color goes on more smoothly.**

Q When I wear gloss, my lips peel and the gloss gets clumpy. What's going on?

A Your lip gloss may have expired! Some glosses are made mostly of petroleum jelly and pigment. Over time, the formula separates and won't keep your lips moisturized. Use a gloss that's water-based or oil-based to help lips retain moisture. It could also be that you have a buildup of dead skin on your lips, so gently buff them with a baby toothbrush once a day.

CG! TIP: Speed the healing of sunburned lips by applying a balm infused with soothing lavender, which may help reduce pain and swelling.

canker sores

Q I keep getting these annoying canker sores. What causes them—and how can I stop from developing them?

A Canker sores are tiny, whitish-red craters that crop up on the tongue, gums, or inside the cheek. They're not dangerous or anything—and with proper care, you can prevent them. Here's how: Cut back on sugary foods, citrus fruits, and coffee, which are all suspected to bring on canker sores. Also, brushing your teeth too hard can cause them, so brush lightly with a soft-bristled brush to avoid irritating your gums. Some antiseptic mouthwashes and tartar-control toothpastes contain chemicals that can irritate the lining of your mouth and cause a sore. Ditching a mouthwash and using an all-natural toothpaste with fluoride may do the trick. Foodwise, not getting enough nutrients—especially folic acid, iron, and vitamin B_{12}—can lead to canker sores, so be sure to get your recommended daily amount of these nutrients. Try eating a bowl of fortified cereal for breakfast, and a sandwich made with whole-wheat bread for lunch. If none of this works, you could try an over-the-counter medicine, like Oragel. It heals the sore by calming the surrounding nerves. Home remedies, such as hot tea, can also lessen pain. If you get canker sores often, see a dentist. She can prescribe a steroid cream to ease the pain.

chapter 6

eye makeup how-tos

Blue, brown, hazel, or green—the eyes are usually what people notice first. In this chapter, we give answers to some of your most pressing questions so you can make your eyes sparkle!

eye makeup how-tos

lush lashes

Q How can I keep my eyelashes curled? By the end of the day, they're always stick-straight. Is it okay to get them permed?

A Definitely not. The chemical solution that's used to perm eyelashes is a slightly watered-down version of regular perm solution, and putting it near your eyes is risky business. Serious damage can occur (even blindness). Besides, once you try this trick from CoverGirl makeup pro B. J. Gillian, you'll never think about perming again. Apply clear mascara to your top lashes, then curl them with an eyelash curler at the roots. Count to 10, then release. Apply one coat of regular mascara to darken your lashes. Skip the second coat, or they'll get too weighed down. Now, go out and flutter that lovely fringe.

Q I've heard that once your eyelashes fall out, they don't grow back—is that true?

A No. Eyelashes, like the hair on your head, fall out and grow back. If your lashes are falling out a lot, you're probably pulling, rather than pinching, with your eyelash curler or rubbing too hard when your eyes itch (or when you're taking off your makeup). In the meantime, a volumizing mascara can help. If all your lashes have fallen out, see a doctor ASAP. Healthwise, something else is probably up (problems with your thyroid or a condition called alopecia areata can cause hair and lash loss).

CG! TIP: **Dot a dark brown liner between the lashes along your top lash lines—it will make them look thicker and define your eyes.**

mascara messes

Q **My mascara always ends up under my eyes. How can I prevent this?**

A Opting for a waterproof formula is the best way to wipe out mascara meltdown (that stuff won't budge until you take it off with eye makeup remover). But if the formula you like isn't waterproof, these tips from MTV makeup artist Kristi Fuhrmann will help: (1) Apply mascara to your top lashes only (the bottom lashes are where most under-eye gunk forms). (2) Use oil-free concealer to cover under-eye circles. (3) Finally, dust a translucent loose powder under your eyes to sop up any excess oil.

Q **I wear clear mascara to avoid raccoon eyes, but it doesn't make my lashes look as full as I'd like. Any tips?**

A You've got two options: Apply gray or brown liner along your top lash line (make it thin), then swipe the clear mascara on your top and bottom lashes. Or try waterproof black-brown mascara on just your top lashes, then put clear on the bottom (where smudging happens).

shadow rules

Q **I love bright eyeshadow! Are there special rules I should follow—like matching my shadow to my shirt?**

A We have a few recommendations when it comes to applying bright eyeshadow. Try dabbing concealer on lids prior to shadow application to make the color stay. Another idea? Try wearing one vivid color at a time. Makeup artist Kris Levine of Christophe Salon in Beverly Hills suggests coral with brown eyes, purple with green eyes, and pink with blue eyes. If you're looking for a more subtle look, trace only your lash line with bright shadow.

CG! TIP: **Sharpen the point of your eyeliner before applying it so it glides smoothly across your lid.**

eye makeup how-tos

Q **My eyeshadow tends to gather in the crease of my eye. Am I doing something wrong?**

A Believe it or not, eyelids produce a lot of oil, so any shadow you apply is basically just sitting on top of a layer of oil. That's why it slides around and ends up concentrated in your crease when you blink. The best thing to do is prep your lids with a base that will soak up oil before you apply shadow. The baselike concealer goes on matte, so it helps shadow stay put. Or you can try this DIY shadow base from Beverly Hills makeup artist Bobbe Joy: Use a makeup sponge (not a brush—the coverage won't be dense enough) to pat loose powder on your lids. Then use a sponge-tip applicator (not your fingers—they'll just add oil) to dab all over your lids a matte powder eye shadow in a shade that matches your skin tone. Powder and powder eye shadows absorb oil, so the color you put over them will stay in place longer. But if you prefer a cream eye shadow, prep lids with loose powder first, then apply the cream over your lids. (You'll need to smooth out the creases every few hours with a fingertip.) Finish with water-resistant mascara, which won't smear or flake.

How can I get that sexy, smoky eye look?

A Getting smoky eyes isn't as hard as it looks. First, line inside your lower rim with a dark brown or black eyeliner. Then, line your upper and lower lash lines, from the inner to the outer corner. Smudge both lines with a cotton swab. Dust a shimmery brown shadow from your lash line to your crease (brown shadow can be just as dramatic as black). Then apply a matte dark brown shadow in just the crease. The outer edge of your shadow should fall between the outer corner of your eye and the end of your brow. The farther out you go, the more dramatic the effect. Finally, use the same matte brown shadow to go over your lash lines again. Finish by cleaning up any stray shadow with a fresh cotton swab and swipe on two coats of mascara.

CGI TIP: **A shiny satin top is the perfect complement to a glam smoky-eye look.**

brow wow

Q I have thin eyebrows. How can I make them look fuller?

A Don't worry—brow powders and pencils are made for this task. If there's no hair at all, use a brow pencil. Choose one that is a shade or two lighter than your natural brow color—it doesn't have to match exactly but don't go any darker. Then sharpen the pencil until it's really sharp and carefully fill in any spaces. To keep your new brows from looking too drawn-in, take a tissue and gently rub it along the shape of your brows. It will instantly look more natural!

Didja Know?
Back in ancient Greece, a unibrow was considered to be a sign of beauty and great intelligence in women.

Q Help—I just overplucked my eyebrows! What can I do?

A Until your brows grow back, try a brow powder to fill in hairless patches and create shape. Don't try to create a new shape with the shadow—just follow your natural one. Do this for about six to eight weeks while your brows grow out, then head to a salon for a brow shaping—it'll cost $20 or more, but it's worth it!

CG! TIP: Cream shadow's reflective finish draws attention to stray brow hairs, so use tweezers to clean up your arches before you apply it.

eye makeup how-tos

eyeliner application

Q I'd like to wear black eyeliner but don't know how to without looking Goth. Can you give me some tips?

A Black eyeliner can be dramatic and sexy, but if applied wrong, you can end up looking like a raccoon. Here are a few steps to get eyeliner right. For school, brush a neutral shadow over your lids. Using black eyeliner, draw a thin line under your lower lashes, from inner to outer corners, extending it slightly at the outer corner. For a date, build on your school look by also lining the top lash lines. Connect the top and bottom lines at the tail's point. For a party, dust a grayish-black eye shadow from your top lashes to your creases. Highlight inner corners by applying a gray gel pencil on top of the shadow. Redust the black shadow along lower lashes and gently smudge with a cotton swab.

> **CG! TIP:** Line the inner rims of your lower lash lines with a peach eye pencil; the liner won't be very noticeable, but it'll make your eyes look bigger and brighter.

eye illusions

Q **My eyes look so far apart. How can I make them appear closer together?**

A Making your eyes look closer together is actually really easy to do, says Carmindy, a New York City makeup artist. It's all about where on your lids you place eye shadow, and how deep or light the shade is. First, use a sponge-tip applicator (you'll get more precise application) to apply a beige-colored powder shadow from the lash line to the brow bone as a shadow base. Then use a darker shade—like charcoal, navy, or forest green—and pat it over the beige shadow from the inside corner of your lid to the middle (just above your pupil), from lash line to crease. Take a lighter shadow (try lavender if you used charcoal, light blue if you used navy, and gold if you used forest green) and apply it from the middle of your lid to the outer corner (lash line to crease). Gently smudge the center of your lid (where the two shadows meet) with a cotton swab so there's no harsh line and finish by coating your top lashes with black mascara. The deep shadow on the inner corner of your lids gives the illusion of "pulling" your eyes closer together. Just what you wanted!

eye makeup how-tos

Q **I wear glasses and you can't see my eye makeup! Do you have any tips?**

A First, get the right glasses. Choose small wire frames with nonreflective lenses—you want people to see your eyes, not the glare of your glasses. To hide any dark circles and brighten your eye area (which makes eye makeup stand out), use your ring finger to pat three to four dots of creamy concealer under your eyes with a shade that's lighter than the skin on your face (if you're circle-free, you can skip this step.) Next, blend a highlighting stick in a shade that matches the skin on your brow, just above your cheekbones. Matte shadows can disappear behind glasses. Shimmery shadows have more texture because they reflect light, so the color will pop out from behind your frames. Wear bright, pastel-colored shades like peach or green. Apply mascara which will make your eyeshadow look more pronounced. Swipe two or three coats on top lashes and apply one coat to your bottom lashes for maximum effect.

bloodshot eyes

Q Lately my eyes look bloodshot. What can I do?

A That all depends on what's causing them to be bloodshot. As a quick fix, squirt eyedrops into each eye. However, if your eye makeup has been irritating them, try avoiding it until the redness clears up. Instead, wear a bold lipstick. It will draw attention to your gorgeous lips instead of your red eyes. If the problem persists for more than two days, be sure to see a doctor to rule out a possible eye infection.

CG! TIP: **Up all night studying? Make your eyes appear more awake by curling your lashes.**

chapter 7

hair help

Hair maintainence is at the top of every CosmoGIRL!'s beauty to-do list and it's no wonder—your hair is your best accessory! So If you suffer from frizz, split ends, or zero volume, don't worry. Read on for the tips you need to love your hair, every day.

dry hair

Q **I have extremely dry hair (it's curly and chemically processed). Any suggestions on which products to use?**

A Curly hair is usually drier than straighter hair, and in your case, the chemical processing weakened your hair's cuticle, making it more vulnerable to dryness, breakage, and split ends. Here are four moisture-boosting tricks: (1) Be extra careful to always use moisturizing hair products, especially shampoo. Some shampoos have harsh detergents that can dry out your curls. Check your bottle and make sure you're buying a shampoo that's labeled "gentle" or "moisturizing," or that is made specifically for curly/chemically processed hair. These shampoos have special moisturizing ingredients your curls need to keep them in the best condition. Don't shampoo more than every two to three days—washing every day will overdry your hair. (2) Have your stylist trim at least an inch off your ends (where your hair is the most dry and damaged) every four to six weeks. (3) In addition to using a conditioner for curly/chemically processed hair whenever you shampoo, twice a week use a deep-conditioning treatment packed with protein. The extra protein will help keep your hair healthy and shiny. Just wash and condition as usual, apply the conditioner from roots to ends, leave it on for about 20 minutes, then rinse out and style.

The ends of my naturally curly hair look dry. Help!

A When you have curly hair, your scalp's moisturizing oils have a hard time winding around and down to the end of your curls. To prevent dryness, always use a moisturizing shampoo and conditioner. Whenever your ends look dry, mist them with water, then smooth your strands from midshaft to end with an oil-based moisturizer.

CG! TIP: **Check out naturallycurly.com for styling tips and the latest trends for curly hair.**

oily hair

Q **I have really oily hair. I wash it every morning—but by the afternoon, it's greasy again. Any suggestions?**

A Don't worry—this plan from Coco Santiago, a stylist at the Bumble and Bumble Salon in New York City, will leave you virtually oil-free: Use a clear shampoo (as opposed to the creamy kind) containing tea tree oil once a day. The tea tree oil balances your scalp's oil production (the same way toner controls the oil on your face). Skip conditioner unless you have long hair—and then use just a light detangler on your ends. Use a clarifying shampoo once a week. When you style, stick to alcohol-based products, like smoothing balm. Try covering up midday grease by sprinkling baby powder on your roots. And finally, try not to touch your hair so much. Constant fiddling spreads dirt and oil from your hands (which have more dirt than you want to know) onto your hair, making it limp.

frizz fighters

Q Before I go to school, my hair looks sleek and straight. But by the time I get there, it's frizzy! How can I make my hairstyle stay all day?

A Blow-dry your hair before bed (sleeping on it tames the poofiness). In the morning, apply a dime-sized blob of smoothing scrum to your hair, from roots to tips. Wear a silk scarf on your head until you get indoors, then remove it. Voilà—frizz-free hair!

CG! TIP: **Towel-dry your hair during the summer to cut down on damage from styling tools. But blot—don't rub—It dry, or you'll end up with the frizzies.**

hair help

Q **I highlighted my hair a month ago for the second time, and now it's so dry and frizzy that I'm afraid to wear it down. What can I do?**

A You've got to start an intensive conditioning routine ASAP. Every time you shampoo, apply a protein-rich deep-conditioning treatment. Leave it on for 15 minutes, then rinse it out and spritz on a leave-in conditioner. Once it looks healthier (it should take two weeks to a month), deep-condition once a week (but still use a regular conditioner made for your hair type and spray on leave-in conditioner after every shampoo). And remember, highlight only every six to eight weeks!

Q I recently used a flat iron on my curly hair, and now it frizzes instead of curls. Did the iron damage my hair?

A If you said you'd been using an iron every day, then yes, your hair might be super-dried-out (and frizzing), says Ouidad, a New York stylist and curly hair specialist. But since it does not sound like you're a regular user, your sudden frizz is probably due less to the styling tool and more to some other habit, like under-conditioning (curly hair needs more moisture than other types) or chemically processing your hair. To help hydrate your hair and flatten frizz, try this: After washing and conditioning, mix (in your hands) a silver-dollar-sized dollop of control gel, a few drops of leave-in conditioner, and a quarter-sized amount of silicone-based defrizzer. Apply to clean, damp hair (run it through with a wide toothed comb), then let your hair air-dry. In addition, deep-condition your hair at least once a week and limit your flat iron usage to special occasions only.

CG! TIP: **Sleep with a bandana or scarf tied around your hair. You'll tame frizz at your roots but get volume at your ends.**

smart styling

Q My hair is always flat. I've tried flipping it upside down and hairspraying it, but that doesn't seem to work. What else can I do?

A Flipping your hair upside down and spraying it makes it stay full for about an hour, but eventually the spray will weigh down your ends and your hair will be even flatter. To get lasting oomph, use a volumizing spray, which gives body to your hair. Divide damp hair into a top and bottom section, and clip the top part up. Blow-dry the bottom section. Then unclip the top part and use a comb to divide it into several 2- to 3-inch sections. Hold each section of hair upward and away from your head and aim the volumizing spray underneath it, at your roots. Keep your hair divided into sections and comb each one with a wide-toothed comb to distribute the spray. Then use a big round brush to lift up each section, one by one, blasting your blow-dryer underneath until your roots are dry (about 10 seconds). But don't pull the brush out yet—leave it in each section for 15 seconds to let your hair cool (this will lock in volume at the roots). Next, holding the dryer nozzle six inches away from the top of your hair, brush through each section until it's dry, keeping your roots lifted as you move the brush (pull hair to the side of your head). That way, you won't flatten the volume you put in.

Q I need a hairstyle that will hide my huge forehead, but I don't want bangs! What can I do?

A Ask your stylist to cut long layers, beginning at your cheekbones and tapering off toward the ends, suggests New York stylist Ouidad. This'll add width to the lower half of your face and draw attention away from your forehead. Also, keep your hair shoulder-length or longer, and wear ponytails at the nape of your neck, not up high.

CG! TIP: **Long, choppy layers add an edge to hair that's shoulder-length or longer, while blunt bangs and subtle layers make even a basic bob look cool and funky.**

hair help

Q **How can I make one of those hair headbands I've seen?**

A It's easier than you think! First, split your hair in half from ear to ear, and clip the bottom chunk out of the way. Divide the top half into two sections—front and back. French braid the front section, starting from the left and finishing on the right. (It's okay if some shorter layers hang out.) Secure with an elastic band. Repeat on the back section, braiding from your right ear to your left. Bobby-pin the tails behind your ears and finish by unclipping the bottom portion of your hair.

CG! TIP: **For a romantic look, tie a piece of lace ribbon around the base of your ponytail.**

Q My hair is short and really thin. How can I make it look fuller?

A Getting thicker-looking strands is as easy as getting one good cut by following these three styling steps, says Mark Garrison, a New York City stylist and owner of the Mark Garrison Salon. First, the cut: Garrison says layers are crucial for adding volume to fine hair. Ask your stylist to create them all over, especially in the back, where hair tends to fall flattest (bringing in a picture of a short cut with the volume you want is also helpful). Now the styling tips: (1) Use a volumizing shampoo followed by a light detangling conditioner. (2) Spritz a body-building spray gel on just the roots of your hair (a little extra lift at the scalp makes the rest of your hair look fuller too). (3) Blow-dry your hair (do most of the work upside down, then flip your head back up to finish), and using a big-barreled curling iron, clamp it to the roots of your hair (in inch-wide sections) and hold for five seconds. Finish by sliding the iron through to the ends, fluff a little with your fingers, and go!

Didja Know?
When it's humid out, moisture in the air can make hair swell up to 15 percent thicker.

hair color clues

Q I want to color my hair for a new back-to-school look, but I don't want it to be obvious. What kind of subtle change can I make that'll still have people saying, "Wow!"?

A Whatever your hair color, there are plenty of cool shades that will perk up your color. If you're brunette, go for deep burgundy highlights. If you're blond, try a light auburn tint and keep your new color intact by using color-enhancing shampoo and conditioner.

CG! TIP: Ask your stylist for a gloss treatment. It will make your hair look and feel instantly shinier and smoother for up to six weeks.

Q **I have dark blond hair and want to dye it so it's brighter and lighter. How should I do it?**

A At your local drugstore, pick up a highlighting kit and have a friend do the highlighting for you (it's too hard to do the back of your head by yourself). She should start on the right (so the highlights are in line with the tip of your right ear) and work around to the left, saving the strands by your face for last. Have her work on sections that are half an inch apart and about the size of a pencil, alternating shades (one dark, one light). She should lift each section, dip the applicator comb in the cream, and run it through, roots to ends. The cream is thick, so it shouldn't drip (but to be sure, have her lay the sections down gently, and don't move your head). When she does the strands by your face, paint them with just the lighter shade. To stay root-free, repeat in eight weeks.

> **CG! TIP: When home-coloring your hair, follow directions exactly. Leaving dye on for too long or not long enough can drastically change the results!**

hair help

Q I have long, thick hair that's been dyed so many times it looks dead. And my roots are starting to show again! What do I do?

A Dyes work by opening up the hair shaft enough to allow color in, and let moisture out. The result? Strawlike strands. The remedy? Put aside your color kit for a little while and treat your tresses to some TLC. Give yourself twice-weekly deep-conditioning treatments to restore some hydration. Coat damp hair with a thick conditioner, wrap your head in plastic wrap, wait for 20 minutes, then rinse. Note: It may take three months to revive really dried-out strands, so hang in there. To treat your roots situation, color only a few pieces around your face to hide the obvious regrowth without leaving your whole head dry.

Q I color my hair on my own. How can I make it look like I went to the salon?

A Did you know that 44 percent of CG!s also color their own hair? Here are some tips to help you out. To avoid mistakes when coloring your hair at home, patch-test a piece of hair at the nape of your neck to see how the dye reacts with your skin and hair before applying it all over. After you color your hair, wait as long as you can (24 to 48 hours) before you shampoo, to give the color time to be absorbed. Always use a shampoo and conditioner formulated for color-treated hair—they won't strip your hair of its color. The sun can also fade your color, so cover your hair if you're going to be in direct sunlight for more than an hour. Also use styling products with UV filters.

hair help

Q **I tried to color my dark brown hair blond, but it's not as light as I want it to be. How long do I have to wait before I can color it again?**

A Going from dark brown to blond is pretty tricky—even for professional colorists. Here's the thing: Most at-home permanent hair-color kits lighten your hair only two to three shades. There are a few kits that can lighten a bit more dramatically, but even those won't turn dark brown hair blond (you'll get more of a light coppery shade instead). Bottom line? How light you can go with a home-color kit depends on the color you start with—so check the shade guide on the box to get an idea of what to expect. Now, if you really want to go lighter, we recommend going to a salon and having a professional colorist finish the job. She'll either do a double-process treatment, or just add blonder highlights on top of the color you already have (a lot of colorists pre-lighten hair before they add any highlights, so by coloring at home, you've already done the first step). Expect to pay between $50 and $200 depending on where you live (urban areas tend to be pricier). And no matter what you do, be sure to deep-condition once a week. Remember: lightened hair = drier hair.

Q I'm considering coloring my hair, but with so many options out there, I'm not really sure what to do. Any advice?

A Here's a rundown to decode "stylist" language and get the look you want. A semi-permanent is a temporary all-over color—it only lasts six to eight shampoos—that won't chemically change your natural pigment. In a single process, a permanent color or bleach is painted over your entire head with a brush so that your color is the same all over. With a demi-permanent, color is temporary and lasts about six to eight weeks. There's no ammonia, but there is peroxide, which helps color stick to your strands. In a double process, all color is stripped from your hair (to create a blank slate), then toner is applied to your bleached strands to make the new color. With highlights, strands or chunks of hair are lightened using foils or painting techniques. Lowlights are similar to highlights, except that your base color is darkened instead of lightened. This process is usually combined with highlights to add dimension. A toner is a light-colored tint that can be applied on top of any process to enhance the tones of newly colored hair by neutralizing brassy or orange color. Now do you know what you want?

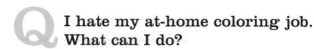
Q I hate my at-home coloring job. What can I do?

A First, call the company's toll-free number and explain what happened. The customer service representative may be able to help. If you used semi-permanent color, you can try to remove it with an at-home treatment. If you used a permanent dye, don't try to fix it yourself—you could make it worse! Make a salon appointment and explain why you are coming in. (They might need to book extra time for a corrective process.) Finally, don't throw out the box. Bring it to the salon to show the colorist what you used and then they can fix it.

Didja Know?

Alcohol in hair products isn't always as bad as you think. The fatty alcohols in conditioners or creams are great moisturizers, and the alcohol in hairspray or spray gel evaporates off your locks before it can do any damage.

hair repair

Q My hair breaks all the time. What can I do?

A When dry, damaged hair gets weak, it eventually separates at the bottom, and the more fragile part breaks off. Have your hair trimmed every six weeks to snip off split ends. Otherwise, they'll split even further up your hair shaft, and when they break you'll lose longer pieces of hair. Also, apply to damp hair a strengthening cream with ceramides before using any heated tools. Ceramides reinforce weak spots and seal the cuticle to help prevent damage.

CG! TIP: **Gently crimpled ends look naturally gorgeous and take much less work to create than perfectly twirled waves.**

hair help

Q **My scalp hurts after I get my hair braided. What can I do?**

A It's normal for your scalp to be a little sore after you get your hair braided. But if the soreness doesn't go away after two days, or tiny bumps appear on your scalp, it could mean the tension from the braids is damaging your hair follicles. If you keep braiding, you could eventually develop traction alopecia—bald spots where the damaged hair no longer grows. To prevent that, undo your braids, leave them out for about two weeks, and use a recovery shampoo and conditioner to nourish your scalp. You can start braiding again (a little more loosely than before), but keep your scalp healthy by wearing braids for a few weeks, then alternating with another style for a week.

Will using a flat iron every day ruin my hair?

A Yes. You should use a flat iron every other day at most, because the process sucks out your hair's natural moisture. When you do flat-iron, use these tips from celebrity hairstylist Nathaniel Hawkins. Coat towel-dried hair with a dime- to quarter-sized amount of silicone-based moisturizing styling product. Blow-dry your hair completely, then glide the hot iron over each section in one quick motion (don't leave it in one place for more than two seconds). Be sure to use a flat iron with ceramic-plated paddles—unlike metal-plated irons, they'll deliver heat to the core of your strands without drying them out.

hair help

Q I use a flat iron every morning, but no matter what I do, I always get short little hairs that stick up around my face. Help!

A It sounds like your hair is breaking from too much exposure to high heat. Prevent further breakage by using a heat-protection spray before you iron. In the meantime, smooth broken hairs with a pea-sized amount of hair wax.

Didja Know?
Hair suddenly hard to style? If you've been using the same shampoo forever, that could be why—so try a new one.

hair loss help

Q **Every time I wash or brush my hair, it falls out! It seems to be getting a lot thinner. What should I do?**

A It's totally normal to lose hair daily. To ease your mind, however, try washing with a sensitive shampoo for fine hair. If you notice you're still losing a lot more than the normal amount (way more than 100 hairs), see your doctor.

hair help

Q **I have long, thick, wavy hair that I've permed three times within the last six months. Last week, it started falling out. What can I do?**

A Don't panic. The hair experts we asked assured us that your hair isn't really falling out—it's just breaking off so close to the root it appears to be coming out of your scalp. Start a deep-conditioning routine immediately, says Damian Santiago, a stylist at the Bumble and Bumble Salon in New York City. Choose an intensive conditioning treatment, and use it at least twice a week (if you have time to do it every other day, that's even better). Then, when you're styling your curls, try to stay away from any heated appliances (like curling irons and blow-dryers) and styling products with high alcohol content (they will dry your hair out even more). In the future, limit your perming to about two to three times per year—and if your curls get droopy in between perms, just get a trim. They'll bounce right back.

Q I wear my hair up in a bun a lot— but I've started to notice that my hairline is receding. How can I stop it?

A It's not permanent, so don't worry. But you do have to give up your bun ASAP. The tension from constantly pulling your hair up in a tight bun is causing a condition called traction alopecia— basically, hair loss from styling stress. (It can also happen if you wear very tight braids or hair weaves.) Trade your bun for a low, loose twist (just make a low ponytail, wrap the hair around the base, and pin it in place with bobby pins). Or try a low ponytail and use bobby pins to hold your front pieces back. The difference with these styles is that they pull the hair down (the way it naturally grows) instead of up, so there isn't nearly as much tension on the roots. You should start to see some regrowth within three months. In the meantime, camouflage your hairline by wearing a thin layer of bangs or a cute head wrap. If your hair doesn't start to come back after three months, see a dermatologist—especially if any other women in your family have hair loss or thinning hair. Your doctor might test you for a nutritional deficiency (not having enough protein or folic acid in your diet can lead to hair loss). But no matter what the cause, your doctor will be able to recommend a treatment that will get your hair back in shape.

hair help

diminishing dandruff

Q **I have really bad dandruff, and it's reached the point where I can't wear anything dark because I get white flakes everywhere. Any advice?**

A It may sound obvious, but using a shampoo designed to get rid of dandruff is really your best bet. Look for one that contains at least one of these FDA-approved ingredients: coal tar, pyrithione zinc, sulphur, or selenium sulfide. All of these additives have been proven to control the fungus that causes dandruff. (Oh, and don't freak—everyone has the fungus. It's just more active on scalps with dandruff.) Once you've found the right shampoo, use it for three days straight (condition like you usually do). Then, if the flakes are gone, start alternating with your regular shampoo. If you don't see results (or you see very little improvement), it's time to see a dermatologist. She can prescribe a medicated scalp treatment that'll quickly get rid of those flakes. Also, make sure you don't have a different flaky/itchy condition like psoriasis or seborrheic dermatitis (they're treatable too, but they're more serious, so you'll need a doctor's help).

black hair how-to's

Q I'm African-American and was wondering if you had styling suggestions for my hair. It seems like there are so many options out there these days, and I have no idea which to choose!

A That all depends on how much time and money you want to spend! For a Malaysian weave, a stylist braids synthetic hair in with your own hair. The process takes about three hours, during which time the stylist will attach 7 to 10 sections of hair. Unlike the bonded weave, this type of weave doesn't use glue (which can damage your hair), and unlike the sew-in weave, the braids aren't lying against your head, so it looks and feels more natural than a sew-in weave. A kiddie perm, intended for kids' hair, straightens the natural texture of your hair. It takes the same amount of time (and costs about the same) as having hair relaxed with a regular-strength relaxer. Because it uses chemicals that are not as strong, a kiddie perm is less damaging to your hair (and less damaging to your scalp) than a relaxer formulated for adults. Sisterlocks are now being used instead of braids. A specially trained stylist creates spaghetti sized strands of hair that you can style in many ways. This unique locking process can take up to 8 to 10 hours. It requires no excessive pulling and no glue, so it doesn't hurt and won't damage your hair or scalp. Sisterlocks are tightened every six weeks so they don't need to be reset.

> **CG! TIP:** **Distribute a dime-sized blob of smoothing serum through a day-old blowout for a carefree, sexy look.**

Didja Know?
An average head of hair is so strong it could support the weight of five small cars. (Of course, don't go and test this at home!)

hair extensions

Q I've been thinking about getting hair extensions, but I'm not sure how to go about it without spending a ton of cash. What can you recommend?

A We recommend clip-in extensions because they can transform any style in minutes and they don't damage hair like bonded extensions can. Go for synthetic clip-ins first; they cost less than human-hair ones. But beware: They'll *melt* if you style them with heated tools!

CG! TIP: **For shiny strands, rub a silk scarf down your hair with a side-to-side motion, roots to ends. (Silk smoothes your hair's cuticles.)**

hair help

salon savvy

Q I'm about to see a professional stylist for the first time. How can I be sure I'll get the style I want?

A No matter your hair type, you need to direct your stylist to get the results you want. Here's how to make sure your new salon and stylist make the cut. When you make the appointment, let them know what type of hair you have (short and curly? long and straight?), then ask for the best stylist for your type. Ask what will happen if you're not happy with the cut and color. A good salon will correct mistakes for free or give you a refund, or both. When you meet a stylist for the first time, ask the receptionist if you can consult with him or her before you're led to the sink to be shampooed. The stylist won't know how your hair will react to what they're suggesting if they haven't seen what it looks and feels like when it's dry. Bring pictures of haircuts you like and don't like so the stylist can get a good idea of the look you're going for. If you're trying a new look—bangs, short hair, etc.—ask the stylist to move your hair around to see what you'll look like. You wouldn't buy an expensive car unless you test-drove it, right? If you're not the type to get frequent haircuts, make sure you and the stylist agree on a cut that won't be too high-maintenance (requiring appointments every six to eight weeks) and don't get color.

If you're uncomfortable with the stylist's suggestions, just say "You know what? Let me think about it before I go through with it." Remember, the stylist doesn't have to live with a bad cut—you do!

CG! TIP: Instead of a traditional pony, try sweeping your hair into a side ponytail—and secure with a beaded elastic. Très chic!

hair help

Q What's the best way to blow out my hair like they do in the salon?

A Wash and condition with a lightweight shampoo and conditioner. Towel-dry your hair, then work a blob (nickel-sized for fine to medium hair, quarter-sized for medium to coarse hair) of a lightweight smoothing cream from midstrand to roots. Use a paddle brush with lots of boar bristles close together and an ionic blow dryer to prevent flyaways. Attach the nozzle and begin drying two-inch sections of your hair, one at a time, starting in the front, near your forehead. If it helps, clip the rest of your hair out of the way. Dry each section with your blow-dryer set on the hottest setting. You may need to run your brush and dryer through each section two to three times to get it perfectly straight and dry. Then remove the heat and allow the section to cool about three to five seconds to set the style before you start the next section.

detangling do's

Q No matter what I do with it, my baby-fine hair always ends up in knots. Help!

A Wash your hair by smoothing shampoo down your strands instead of piling hair on top of your head. Dry your hair by squeezing it—not rubbing—with a soft towel. Use a wide-toothed comb to ease out knots. Start combing down, at the ends, then comb longer strokes until you reach the roots. Combing from ends to roots is actually how you create tangles!

hair help

concealing cowlicks

Q I have a cowlick at the back of my hair that's been there as long as I can remember. Why is it there—and, more importantly, how can I get rid of it?

A A cowlick is a section of hair that sticks up and grows in the opposite direction of the rest of your hair. Sorry, but you can't permanently get rid of it because your hair will always grow that way. You *can* tame the cowlick, however, by having it chemically relaxed at a salon. The stylist will straighten the cowlick so it lies flat on your head. Strategic relaxing is less expensive than an all-over treatment ($50 and up, as opposed to $200 and up), and you'll only need touch-ups twice a year. Too extreme? Try combing wet hair so your cowlick lies flat (in its opposite direction). Then work a dime-sized blob of strong-hold gel through the area to weigh it down. Use a flat brush to brush it in the same direction as you combed it while wet—and then blow-dry hair.

too-short bangs

Q I cut my bangs right after I got out of the shower, and now they're too short. Help!

A Create a deep side part and sweep your bangs as much to one side as you can. Tousle the rest of your hair with a dab of shine serum. It will add texture and give the impression that the short pieces are on purpose. If the side part and textured style don't help disguise your short fringe, see a hairstylist. Ask her to cut a long, thin layer of bangs that'll fall on top of your old ones—the new layer will camouflage your too-short bangs until they grow in (which will take about three to four weeks). If you don't feel like going to a salon (or you've got a cropped cut that won't allow for a new layer), slick your bangs to the side with pomade and a cool clip. Next time, cut bangs on dry, not wet, hair.

CG! TIP: Didn't like how your new shampoo worked on your hair? Don't toss it! Save it and use it to hand-wash your bras and underwear.

chapter 8

nail know-how

Whether you like your nails short or long, polished or bare, nail upkeep is crucial. Here are a few tips on how to keep your fingers and toes looking clean and pretty!

manicure tips

Q How can I get a salon-quality manicure at home?

A First, shape your nails with the rough filing side of a nail buffer so they're square with rounded edges. Smooth any ridges with the fine buffing side. Next, mix 1 tbsp olive oil and 1 cup warm water in a bowl. Soak nails for three minutes to soften cuticles, then afterward, push them back with a manicure stick. Massage hand cream from your cuticles to your wrists in circular motions. Then clean nails with polish remover (polish lasts longer on clean nails). Finally, apply a clear base coat, then paint on two coats of color from nail base to tip. Follow with a clear top coat to prevent chipping and add shine.

Didja Know?
Your fingernails grow faster in warm weather and right before your period.

---

nail fixes

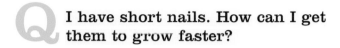

Q I have short nails. How can I get them to grow faster?

A Nails have to be strong to grow. These tips should do the trick: Every day, rub hand lotion into your cuticles to moisturize skin. A strong cuticle protects the new, growing nail. Once a week, coat nails with a clear strengthening polish to protect nails from wear and tear. File tips into a squarish shape (pointy nails are weaker). Then apply two coats of colored polish.

Didja Know?
Quick-dry top coats make nail polish chip faster— so save them for when you're really rushed.

nail know-how

Q **My nails are peeling. What can I do to make them stronger?**

A Keep your cuticles and nails hydrated by massaging olive oil into them. Also, once a week, use a strengthening polish. When removing nail color, use an acetone-free polish remover—it won't dry out your nails. Also, a common cause of brittle nails is iron deficiency, so make sure you eat some lean meat or leafy greens daily.

CG! TIP: **Don't want to leave the beach with sand stuck to your toes? Sprinkle sandy feet with a little baby powder—it soaks up moisture so the sand brushes off more easily.**

Q My toenails are yellow and my feet itch all the time. It's so annoying and gross. What should I do?

A Sounds to us like a case of athlete's foot! Want a good natural remedy to soothe the itching? Try using raw garlic. The oils from raw, fresh garlic will reduce the itch and may even help kill the fungus. Take one clove of garlic and cut it in half. Rub the garlic over the infected areas of your foot, between and around your toes. Leave on the juices for 30 minutes, then rinse with warm water and dry thoroughly. Do this once a day for a week. In the meantime, while you're healing, always dry in between your toes after showering and change your socks at least once a day. Also, avoid wearing the same pair of shoes every day. You want to give your shoes a little more time than that to "air out" before wearing them. If the garlic remedy doesn't work—or if you're not willing to rub garlic all over your feet!—there are lots of over-the-counter remedies for athlete's foot, all of which take four weeks to get rid of the itchy foot fungus.

index

A

Acne, 44–59
African-American skin
and, 19, 21
aspirin for, 54
bad, treatment, 49, 56
before/after period, 46
blackheads, 57
on chest, 58
combination skin and,
17
concealing, 18, 54,
55
dark spots after, 21
easing into regimen, 50
eliminating without
drying skin, 50
how medicines work,
47
ingredients in
medicines, 13, 21,
47–48, 50, 51
medications by skin
type, 13
mild, treatment, 49
oily skin and, 15–16
oozing pimples, 55
percent of active
ingredients, 51
preventing pimples, 46
putting off treating, 53
quick fixes, 54
reducing redness, 55
scars, concealing, 65
on shoulders, 59
talking with parents
about, 53
tanning and, 28
tea tree oil for, 48
time for treatment
results, 50
toothpaste for, 52
treating before pimple
appears, 46
African-American hair,
119–120
African-American skin
acne and, 19, 21
bleaching creams and,
19
cleansing, 19, 21
dark spots on, 21
Armpits
dark shadowy
appearance, 43
deodorant for, 26, 42
shaving, 42–43
Asian skin, foundation
matching, 63
Aspirin, 54

index

Astringents, 14, 17
Athlete's foot, 133

B

Benzoyl peroxide cleanser,
    18, 46, 47, 49,
    50, 59
Bikini line, 39–40
Blackheads
    in ears, 57
    what they are, 57
Bleaching creams, 21,
    25
Bloodshot eyes, 91
Blowing out hair, 124
Braces, for teeth, 73
Breasts, stretch marks on,
    25
Burned skin, preventing
    scars, 20

C

Canker sores, 77
Carmindy, 89
Chapped lips
    preventing, 75
    treating, 75
Cleansing tips, 12–14
    acne and. See Acne

African-American skin,
    19
combination skin, 17
generic vs. brand-name
    products, 12
getting shimmery skin,
    33
number of products to
    use, 13
sensitive skin, 18–19
tingly feel or not, 12
toners vs. astringents,
    14
Coloring hair, 104–110
    brightening dark blond,
        105
    from dark brown to
        blond, 108
    demi-permanants,
        109
    do-it-yourself look, 107
    drying out hair, 106
    fixing bad job, 110
    highlighting kits, 105
    highlights and lowlights,
        109
    semi-permanents, 109
    subtle effects, 104
    toners, 109
    touching up roots, 106

types of treatments, 109
Combination skin, 17
Concealing
  acne scars, 65
  cowlicks, 126
  foundation basics,
    62–63
  freckles, 67
  hair cowlicks, 126
  pimples, 18, 54–55
  razor burn, 41
  sunburn, 66
  undereye circles, 64
Cowlicks, 126

D

Dandruff, 118
Dark spots, on skin, 22
Deodorant, 26, 42, 43
Dinehart, Scott, 48

E

Ears, blackheads in, 57
Electrolysis, 38
Exfoliating, 23, 32
Eye illusions
  glasses and, 90
  hiding bloodshot eyes,
    91

looking closer together,
  89
looking more awake,
  91
seeing makeup through
  glasses, 90
sexy, smoky look,
  85
Eyes, 78–91
  bloodshot, 91
  circles under,
    concealing, 64
  eyelashes falling out,
    81
  eyeliner application,
    88
  eye shadow rules and
    tips, 83–85
  filling in hairless brow
    patches, 87
  fuller brows, 86
  lines and wrinkles
    around, 24
  lush lashes, 80–81
  mascara, 82, 84, 85
  overplucking brows,
    87
  perms for eyelashes,
    80
  thicker lashes, 81

index

F

Facial hair, 38
Fading creams. *See*
    Bleaching creams
Flossing teeth, 71
Foundation
    Asian skin and, 63
    hiding freckles with,
        67
    pale skin and, 62
Freckles, concealing,
    67
Fuhrmann, Kristi, 82

G

Garrison, Mark, 103
Generic vs. brand-name
    products, 12
Gillian, B.J., 80
Glycolic acid, 16, 47, 57
Grossman, Karyn, M.D.,
    25

H

Hair, 93–127
    adding volume to,
        100, 103
    African-American, tips,
        119
    bangs too short, 127
    blowing out, 124
    blunt bangs, 101
    braiding, soreness
        after, 112
    breaking, 114
    buns causing receding
        hairlines, 117
    coloring. *See* Coloring
        hair
    cowlicks, concealing,
        126
    curly, with dry ends,
        95
    dandruff, 118
    dry, treating, 94–95, 98
    extensions, 121
    fine, tangling, 125
    flat irons and,
        113–114
    flat, making fuller, 100
    frizz fighters, 97–99
    fuller looking, 100
    gloss treatment, 104
    headband of, 102
    hiding high forehead,
        101
    long, choppy layers,
        101
    losing, 115–116

Malaysian weave, 119
oily, treating, 96
removing. *See* Hair
    removal
repairing, 111–114
shampoo and conditioner
    for, see *specific*
    conditions
stylists, tips on working
    with, 122–123
tangled, 125
Hair removal, 35–43
    aloe vera soothing,
        39
    armpits, 42–43
    avoiding stubble, 37
    bikini line, 39–40
    bleaching instead of,
        38
    bumps after shaving,
        41, 42
    dark shadowy under
        arms and, 43
    electrolysis, 38
    facial hair, 38
    for heavy growth,
        36
    plucking, 36
    pubic hair, 39–40
    razor burn and, 41

    shaving, 36, 37,
        40–41
    using depilatory for, 36,
        37
    waxing, 36, 37, 38, 39,
        40
Hawkins, Nathaniel,
    113
Hickey, treating, 22
Hydrocortisone, 42, 49,
    54

J

Jaliman, Debar, 37

L

Levine, Kris, 83
Lines
    around eyes, 24
    red, on breasts, 25
Lips and mouth. *See also*
    Teeth
    canker sores, 77
    chapped lip treatment,
        75
    clumpy gloss, 76
    fuller-looking lips, 74
    lip balm before make
        up, 75

index

mouthwash, 71
preventing chapped
    lips, 75
treating sunburned lips,
    76

M

Makeup. *See also*
    Foundation
    combination skin and,
        17
    for eyes. *See* Eyes
    lip balm before, 75
    oily skin and, 15–16
Malaysian weave, 119
Manicures. *See* Nails
Mascara, 82, 84–85
Mouth. *See* Lips and
    mouth; Teeth
Murad, Howard, M.D.,
    54

N

Nails, 129–133
    growing faster,
        131
    peeling, 132
    quick-dry nail polish,
        131
    salon-quality home
        manicure, 130
    strengthening, 132
    yellow toenails and
        itchy feet, 133
Nutrition
    healthy fats for skin,
        22
    preventing canker
        sores, 77

O

Oily hair, 96
Oily skin, 15–16
    acne medications for,
        13
    combination skin and,
        17
    feeling greasy after
        washing, 16
    makeup running, 15

P

Paul, Sabrina B., 33
Perms
    for eyelashes, 80
    for hair, causing hair
        loss, 115
Pimples. *See* Acne

Plucking 36, 87
Pores
    blackheads and, 57
    cleaning. *See* Cleansing
        tips
    large, 23
Preventing
    canker sores, 77
    chapped lips, 75
    lines and wrinkles, 24
    pimples, 46
    scars, 20
Pubic hair, removing, 39,
    40

R

Razor burn, 41
Roncal, Mally, 63
Rosenthal, Larry, D.D.S.,
    72

S

Salicylic acid, 18, 19, 21,
    46, 47, 50, 51, 58, 59
Santiago, Coco, 96
Santiago, Damian, 116
Scars
    concealing, 65
    keeping from darkening,
        21
    preventing, 20

Schick, Morgen, 62
Self-tanners, 30–33
    blotchy look with, 31
    choosing right color, 32
    DHA in, 32
    exfoliating before using,
        31
    model regimen, 33
    reducing scent of, 32
    removing from hands,
        31
    staining things, 30–31
    turning skin orange,
        32
Sensitive skin
    African-American skin,
        19
    cleansing, 18, 19
    irritation after shaving,
        41–43
Shaving. *See* Hair removal
Shimmery skin, 33
Sisterlocks, 119–120
Skin. *See also* Sensitive
    skin
    cleansing. *See*
    Cleansing tips
    combination, 17
    hickey on, 22
    large pores, 23

index

lines and wrinkles on,
24
oily, 15–16
preventing scars, 20
protecting from UV rays,
26, 27
shimmery, 33
Stretch marks, 25
Sun, 26–29
acne and tanning,
28
harmful effects of,
26–27
occasional sunbathing,
27
preventing lines and
wrinkles, 24
protecting from UV rays,
24
self-tanners instead of,
30–33
sunscreen for. See
Sunscreen
tanning beds and,
26
Sunburn
base tan and, 27
concealing, 66
on lips, healing, 76
Sunscreen, 29

to avoid wrinkles/lines,
24
to keep scars from
darkening, 20–21
shelf life of, 29
SPF level to use, 24,
29
sunscreen for, 29
UV protection, 24, 29
when to apply/reapply,
29

T

Tanning. See Self-tanners;
Sun
Tanning beds, 26
Tea tree oil, 48
Teeth
bad, fixing, 70
braces for, 73
brushing, 71
flossing, 71
treatment costs, 70
whitening, 72
Toners, 14, 17, 23
Toothpaste
for acne, 52
irritating mouth, 71
whitening, tooth color
and, 72

U

Underarms. *See* Armpits

V

Vitamin C, for lines/
    wrinkles, 24
Vitamin E cream, 20

W

Waxing hair, 36–40
Whitening teeth, 72
Wisch, Peter, 52
Wrinkles, 24